Presented To

_____

By

_____

Date

_____

THE
POCKET DEVOTIONAL
FOR TEENS

Honor Books
Tulsa, Oklahoma

The Pocket Devotional for Teens
ISBN 1-56292-876-7

Copyright © 2002 by Honor Books, Inc.
P.O. Box 55388
Tulsa, Oklahoma 74155

Compiled and written by Marcia Ford

Introduction

Everyone says, "Take time to read your Bible. Study the wisdom that has stood the test of time." But *time* is a test for you, too, right? Who can find the time with all the exams and reading assignments, not to mention the job after school? Well, here is a solution for you—a devotional that collects challenging scriptures and also provides life-changing reflections and astute quotations to go with each one. This winning combination will help you experience the kinds of changes in your life that will make you the kind of person you long to be, to help you reach your highest dreams.

Carry it in your backpack or bag to use in that spare moment at lunchtime or just before the bell rings. Tuck it by your bedside for that last thought before sleep hits or for the first thought before the business of the day hits. *The Pocket Devotional for Teens* will give you that spiritual lift to get you through your busy day and into the future.

Sweet is a grief
well ended.

*The LORD is close to the
brokenhearted, and he
saves those whose spirits
have been crushed.*

PSALM 34:18 NCV

Brokenhearted Blues

When our hearts have been shattered, we can't imagine a time when they will ever be whole again. We lie in bed at night, staring at the ceiling as we choke back the tears and struggle to breathe. The emotional pain is so intense that we usually end up in physical pain as well. Pieces of our hearts seem to be gone forever.

If you're among the brokenhearted, you can find comfort in the promise that your spirit can be restored and your heart can be put back together again. All you have to do is hand the whole works over to God. That means every bit of it, even those things you'd like to hold on to—like misery. Feeling miserable often beats risking further disappointment, but if you're going to trust God to fix this situation, you'll have to trust Him completely.

Be as careful with another person's heart as God is with yours.

He hath no leisure
who useth it not.

Martha was upset over all the work she had to do so she came and said, "Lord, don't you care that my sister has left me to do all the work by myself? Tell her to come and help me!" The Lord answered her, "Martha, Martha! You are worried and troubled over so many things, but just one is needed. Mary has chosen the right thing, and it will not be taken away from her."

LUKE 10:40-42 TEV

Crash, Boom, Burn

Are you one of the kids who's bordering on schedule overload? You know one type: those heavily involved in sports activities, serving in the student government, volunteering for fund-raisers, and working toward a 4.0 GPA. Then there's another type: those struggling to get homework done because of having to work as much as possible and then help out with the housework and younger siblings in their single-parent households. One is active by choice, the other by necessity.

One thing's for sure: if you're one of either type of those kids and you don't take time out to renew your mind and restore your spirit, you're going to suffer–big time. So will all the things you are responsible for. Even if you seem to have limitless energy, you're going to end up snapping at people and making a mess of things if you don't stop and take care of yourself.

Rest each day–spend some time in deep thought about your life.

All work is as seed sown;
    it grows and spreads,
    and sows itself anew.

*Fixing our eyes on Jesus . . .
    who for the joy set before
    Him endured the cross . . .
and has sat down at the right
    hand of the throne of God.*

HEBREWS 12:2 NASB

Go for the Goal

Maybe your prospects for the future don't look that bright. But one of the most brilliant men who ever lived—Jesus Christ—believes you have just as good a shot at success as a classmate planning a career in medicine.

The key is to have a goal. Couple that with a clear and steady gaze at the One who stands at the finish line, and you have a winning combination.

If you don't have a specific goal in life, now's the time to set one—just make sure you don't set it in stone. Always be open to change, especially a change in direction that you feel certain is from God. If you approach your goal one step at a time, paying close attention to the spiritual signposts along the way, you're sure to end up just where God wants you to be.

Never let anyone convince you that you can't be what God says you can be.

I used to be angry every day;
now every other day; then
every third or fourth day;
and if you miss it so long as
thirty days, offer a sacrifice
of thanksgiving to God.

*It is better to be patient than
powerful. It is better to
win control over yourself
than over whole cities.*

PROVERBS 16:32 TEV

Drivers Ed

Don't you hate it when other drivers cut you off in traffic? You want to lay on the horn and give them a piece of your mind. There is always some jerk ready to side-swipe you, all because he wants to show off his wheels!

Slow down. The worst thing you can do with a jerk is join his ranks. Don't even let him know he got you all riled up inside. Just wave–OK, just a half-wave–and go on your way, replacing your vengeful thoughts with something else, like your weekend plans. Dwelling on the incident will only ruin your day, and that other driver has already taken more of your time than he deserves.

Letting go of potential road rage confrontations is one example of ruling your spirit. The next step–praying for the driver–is a huge step toward maturity.

Don't let the foolishness of others sideswipe you on your way to responsible living.

Little said is
soon amended.

*Their stupidity will be evident
even to strangers they meet
along the way; they let everyone
know that they are fools.*

ECCLESIASTES 10:3 TEV

Jingle Bells

Remember the last time you opened your mouth and wished you hadn't? It happens to everybody—even presidents, rock stars, and pastors. The funny thing is that most of the time a tiny little alarm goes off in our heads. It's saying, "Don't go there!"—but all too often, our mouths are already open, and the comments come tumbling out way too fast.

There are a few tricks to avoiding this: One is to wait until you're sure you want to say what you're about to say—and then wait some more. That slight delay could make all the difference in whether or not you hurt someone or make a fool of yourself. A second trick is to turn up the volume on the alarm by paying closer attention to it each time it rings. After a while, you'll begin to hear it loud and clear.

*Alarms go off for a reason—
learn to listen to them.*

Most wondrous book!
Bright candle of the Lord!

*Your word is a lamp
to guide me and a
light for my path.*

PSALM 119:105 TEV

Basic Training

Maybe you've heard the stories from your parents—the countless Christmas Eves they were up all night trying to assemble a bike, a dollhouse, or some other complicated gift they purchased when you were a child. Some parents foolishly try to put things together without reading the instructions, but others find that even when they do try to follow the directions, the assembly guide is incomplete.

That's what sets the Bible apart as an instruction guide for life: It was written by God himself, using human writers to explain to us all we need to know about making a go of it on planet Earth. It is the guidebook for life. As you read it, life begins to make more sense and you discover more and more about the best way to live so that your time on Earth will be better spent.

Surf the Net or ask a bookstore staff person for help in finding a good Bible version.

I see not a step before me
as I tread on another year;
But I've left the Past in
God's keeping—the Future
His mercy shall clear.

*If we are faithless, he will
remain faithful, for he
cannot disown himself.*

2 TIMOTHY 2:13

Which Way Is Up?

It's amazing how faithful God is, even when we make decisions that take us from His will. Sometimes we decide to do things that are completely contrary to His nature–things that we know would not please Him. Other times, we make seemingly right decisions that are out of line with what He wants for us. For example, it would seem perfectly reasonable to think that God wants you to enroll in Bible college, but it could be that He wants you to go to a secular campus for an entirely different mission.

If we do make mistakes, does that mean that we've wasted the time we spent off course? No. God is in the business of using everything we've ever experienced to develop our character–to draw us closer to Him. He is so incredibly faithful, creative, and powerful that He can turn our messes into masterpieces.

Give God your mistakes–then sit back and watch His faithfulness go to work.

Better make a weak
man your enemy
than your friend.

*Keep company with the wise
and you will become wise. If
you make friends with stupid
people, you will be ruined.*

PROVERBS 13:20 TEV

The Friendship Factor

Do your parents always get on your case about the kids you hang around with? Maybe they don't want you to have any friends who aren't Christians, have long hair, or are from certain parts of town. Have your friendships become a power struggle?

But this is not about power. In a sense, it's not even about your friends. It's about your *life* and the way you want it to go. The things you do now—the decisions you make today—will have an astonishing effect on you for years to come, far more than you can possibly realize. Lots of people live with regret over the things they did with their friends when they were teenagers. It may be hard to imagine now, but it's true that your friends today can affect the quality of your life tomorrow.

You know whether or not your friends are a good influence—choose them wisely.

He profits most
who serves best.

"Do for others what you want them to do for you: this is the meaning of the Law of Moses and of the teachings of the prophets."

MATTHEW 7:12 TEV

The Golden Rule Rules

We all are familiar with the golden rule—"Do unto others as you would have others do unto you"—but as with many well-known sayings, we don't give it very much thought. When we do think about it, it's usually because someone has broken the rule and we're the victims. But maybe it's time to think about this quote frontwards instead of always backwards—you know—the *do unto others* part.

Doing things for other people often means spending more time serving others—helping your kid sister with her homework, visiting your grandmother in a nursing home, mowing the grass for a handicapped neighbor—which means having less time for ourselves. And that thought doesn't always go over too well. But the people you help will probably never forget your acts of kindness, and the good feeling you'll get as a result will last a lifetime.

No genuine act of kindness
ever goes unrewarded.

Where two discourse,
if the one's anger rise,
the man who lets the
contest fall is wise.

*Do everything without
complaining or arguing.*

PHILIPPIANS 2:14 TEV

Yap, Yap, Yap

Yap (v)—to make a sharp, shrill bark. Some people! They'd complain about anything—it's too hot, it's too cold, you're too late, you're too early. Hopefully, you're not like *that,* but if you're human, chances are you throw out a few complaints of your own: "That pop quiz was unfair;" "My boss treats me like a kid;" "We never do anything interesting in youth group."

Maybe you're right about all those things. But you can't control your teacher, your boss, your parents, or anyone else for that matter; so it doesn't do any good to complain. Look instead at what you *can* do: Keep up with your schoolwork, so you can ace even an unfair quiz. Be the best worker, no matter how your boss treats you. Come up with some cool activities for your youth group. Do what you can, and you'll find you have a lot less to complain about.

You'll be amazed at how your life improves once you stop complaining about it.

Those whose conduct
gives room for talk
are always the first to
attack their neighbors.

*No one who gossips can be
trusted with a secret, but
you can put confidence in
someone who is trustworthy.*

PROVERBS 11:13 TEV

Zip It!

You don't have to live very long before you find out how often your friends repeat secrets you've told them, or maybe you've been the friend who did the repeating. Most of us are guilty of gossip to some degree.

Spreading the news about a medical problem or a classmate's pregnancy before she's told her parents—or the child's father—is the kind of gossip that can destroy relationships. If we don't learn to zip our lips about less important situations, it becomes all too easy to thoughtlessly repeat information—some of it true, some of it untrue—that could cause severe and lasting harm to someone else.

Let your friends know that you can be trusted by not putting down or gossiping about other kids. The more you keep your own mouth closed, the more likely it is that other kids won't talk about you either.

Spreading rumors says more about you than the one whose tale you're telling.

Let thy speech be
better than silence,
or be silent.

*These proverbs can even add to
the knowledge of the wise and
give guidance to the educated.*

PROVERBS 1:5 TEV

Keyword: Silence

You've been hearing it all your life, people—especially your parents—saying, "Just listen to me!" Genuine listening, it seems, is an acquired skill. If you don't believe that, just answer this question: Have you ever been with someone who was talking to you, but when you walked away you realized you had no clue what the person said—because you really weren't listening? Case closed. The guilty verdict is in.

Silence is an even harder skill to master. We all love to talk, and we all love to hear ourselves talk. But if we would quiet down the noise in our brains and listen to the silence, we would come closer to discovering the treasure in others and even our own true selves. Our souls have more to say than we've been able to hear.

Spend a day brushing up on your listening skills—and see how much you learn!

Idleness and lack of
occupation are the best
things in the world
to ruin the foolish.

*Be careful then how you live,
not as unwise people but as
wise, making the most of the
time, because the days are evil.*

EPHESIANS 5:15-16 NRSV

Goal + Time = Success

Here's a secret to ending up at the front of the pack: Do something every day that will bring you closer to your goal in life. It doesn't have to be all that much. But if you exchange one pointless activity—say, a half-hour sitcom—for one productive activity like reading the Bible or a book related to your dreams, you'll enter college or the business world with an incredible amount of knowledge and wisdom.

Take a look at the last twenty-four hours. Were there any time-wasters in there? Those things add up over the course of a week or a month. Now look at the next twenty-four hours. What can you do to make them more satisfying and fulfilling? You own that time, at least the portion of it that's not given to responsibilities at home or outside obligations like work and school. Make your time count.

Keep your eye out for time-robbing habits that you can eliminate from your day.

Count each affliction,
whether light or grave,
God's messenger sent
down to thee; do thou with
courtesy receive him.

*You know that when your faith
succeeds in facing such trials, the result
is the ability to endure. But be sure
that your endurance carries you all the
way without failing, so that you may be
perfect and complete, lacking nothing.*

JAMES 1:3-4 TEV

Pressure Explosion

Do you wish the real world would just stop hassling you, as Matchbox Twenty puts it? We all do, but give it up—it's not going to happen. The real world, with all its hassles, isn't going anywhere soon.

One way to deal with it is to realize how important pressure is to our growth and maturity. We like to think that if we could eliminate all the pressure from our lives, we would be happy, healthy, wealthy, and wise. But that's just not true. We need a certain amount of pressure to push ourselves out of the ruts into which we find ourselves falling. Pressure is what turns a lump of coal into a diamond.

You can also hand those pressures over to God, especially the overwhelming ones that don't seem to be accomplishing much. They probably are, but it's only when they've been placed into His hands that they can be transformed into something good.

Would you rather become a diamond— or remain a lump of coal?

Pure and simple, faith
not lived every day is
not faith; it is facade.

*We are not of those who
shrink back to destruction,
but of those who have faith
to the preserving of the soul.*

HEBREWS 10:39 NASB

Feed Your Faith

Feed your faith? What on earth does that mean? Maybe it sounds like religious jargon, but it really does make a lot of sense. To keep up your physical energy, what should you do? Give it some high-quality nourishment, of course. So what is food for your faith?

Well, first there's the Bible; the words contained in it provide nourishment, giving you spiritual energy and preventing your faith in God from wasting away. Then there's your personal history with God, the things He's done for you or that you've seen Him do for others. Those incidents are like a stockroom from which you can pull out a reminder of His faithfulness when your trust is starting to sag a bit. Finally, there are all those great Christian CDs and books that can fill your head and your heart with the truth about who God is. Chow down!

Make sure you don't feed your faith with junk food!

Accustom yourself to the wonderful thought that God loves you with a tenderness, a generosity, and an intimacy that surpasses all your dreams.

"I have told you this so that you will have peace through your union with me. The world will make you suffer. But be brave! I have defeated the world!"

Ripped Up and Spit Out

Remember the time when the person you had been dating broke up with you or your father left home to start another family or your grandmother died? There's little that other people can do to console you when you feel shattered and ripped apart. What's worse, some people don't even try; they make you feel as if your loss is no big deal. "There are plenty of others to date;" "Everybody's divorced now anyway;" "Well, your grandmother was old."

When there seems to be no one around to hold you and let you cry, remember that the Lord is still the best friend you'll ever have. No, He won't be there in the flesh, but He's as close as your next tear, your next prayer, or your next memory of that loss. Ask Him to comfort you and make himself more real to you—He *will* do it.

When you're grieving, Jesus is the best friend you could possibly have.

The world is large when weary leagues two loving hearts divide. But the world is small when your enemy is loose on the other side.

"I tell you: love your enemies and pray for those who persecute you."

MATTHEW 5:44 TEV

Love Rules

Quick—who's the meanest person you know? Maybe it's that old guy down the street who gives you a dirty look every time he sees you. Or the storeowner who eyes you as if you're about to rob her blind. What are you supposed to do about people like that? Can you say, "Love them"?

Being a teenager is all too often the same thing as being a suspect. It's unfair, but lots of people automatically believe you're up to no good just because of your age. Well, get back at them—love them until it hurts! Heap blessings and good deeds upon them, keep praying for them. They need the love of God more than you could ever imagine. Do they deserve it? No way! Thankfully, God doesn't go by who deserves love. He has decided to love us all.

Turn the tables on those who think you're up to no good by doing good to them.

To have faith is to believe
the task ahead of us is
never as great as the
power behind us.

We live by faith,
not by sight.

2 CORINTHIANS 5:7

Radical Risk Taking

You're no doubt surrounded every day by kids who take risks—some good, some bad. You've probably taken more than a few risks yourself. As a teenager, you're at a point in your life when you're most likely to take risks—and that's not a bad thing, as long as they're worthwhile.

So what's a worthwhile risk? Taking God at His word, for one thing. Lots of people say they do, but their lives don't offer any evidence of that. Do you really believe that you can do all things through Christ? Or that there's a whole world out there that we can't see? The spiritual dimension is there, but it takes eyes of faith to see it. That means seeing what God *can* do rather than what you *see* now. It's a risk worth taking for life.

Faith is often like hiking a trail at night, with only a flashlight to guide your steps.

It isn't the experience of Today that drives men mad. It is the remorse of what happened Yesterday and fear of what Tomorrow might bring. These are God's Days . . . Leave them to Him.

Throw all your worries on him, for he cares for you.

1 PETER 5:7 TEV

Worry Wart

Here's a test to determine if your problems are big enough to worry about: If you think they're too insignificant to pray about, then they're too insignificant to worry about. And if something is big enough to worry about, then it's time to let go of it and give it to God.

Start by defining exactly what the problem is. Maybe you've been grounded for life. You know that's not the real issue, however. The real issue is your relationship with your parents. Ask for specific help in figuring out what you can do to repair what's broken—even if you don't think you're the one responsible for it. Give that relationship to God, do what you can to fix it, and let the rest go. Then stop worrying about it because it's as safe as it can be—held tight in the hands of God. That's casting your cares upon Him.

God cares about your problems
even more than you do.

Those who dream by day
are cognizant of many
things which escape those
who dream only by night.

*A nation without God's
guidance is a nation without
order. Happy are those
who keep God's law!*

PROVERBS 29:18 TEV

I Double Dog Dare You to Dream!

The world is filled with people who have allowed their dreams to die. All around you are people who have settled for second best, people who gave up too soon, maybe before they ever really started pursuing the big dream they had. When their dreams died, so did a part of their souls.

What's your dream for your life? What do you want your life to look like in five, ten, or twenty years? If that's too much to think about, what do you want your life to look like *next* year?

Your dreams will change over the course of your life; that doesn't mean you shouldn't continue to dream. Go after the vision you have now; if it changes in midstream, you at least know what it takes to make your desires a reality. Let God help you make your dreams come true.

Never think you're too young— or too old—to dream big dreams.

When Zeno was asked
what a good friend was,
he replied, "Another I."

*A fool finds no pleasure in
understanding but delights
in airing his own opinions.*

PROVERBS 18:2

Friends That Make You Say, "Hmmm"

Have you ever met people who were so full of themselves that you ended up walking away, shaking your head? Yuck! Being wrapped up in ourselves not only makes a small package but also an unattractive one. People like that can seldom maintain lasting friendships; they bounce around from one group of kids to another. It's no wonder—who wants to be friends with people like that?

Being wrapped up in others means listening to them, giving them opportunities to share their hopes, dreams, fears, and sadness. It means being there for them. It means caring enough to offer support, encouragement, comfort, and even a shoulder or two to cry on—getting at the heart of who they really are, understanding what makes them tick. It means developing deep and abiding relationships, the kind that will survive long after graduation day.

Your time and interest are incomparable gifts to others.

His best companions,
innocence and health;
And his best riches,
ignorance of wealth.

Some people pretend to be
rich, but have nothing.
Others pretend to be poor,
but own a fortune.

PROVERBS 13:7 TEV

For Richer or Poorer

There's nothing wrong with being rich; many a believer has been blessed financially. It's only when wealth becomes the center of our lives that it becomes "the root of all evil." People who use money for all the wrong purposes, no matter how wealthy they may appear, are bankrupt—spiritually and emotionally. They have nothing to present to God and other people. Their money can't buy a soul at peace with God.

Meanwhile, on the other side of the tracks, some of the poorest people have emotional and spiritual bank accounts that are filled to overflowing. They possess the kind of wealth they can never earn. Their riches are found in the peace, joy, praise, and love they experience every day of their lives. What's more, they have riches awaiting them even after they leave this life.

Focus on building up your spiritual account, and the money will take care of itself.

Forgiveness is better than revenge.

"If you forgive others the wrongs they have done to you, your Father in heaven will also forgive you. But if you do not forgive others, then your Father will not forgive the wrongs you have done."

MATTHEW 6:14-15 TEV

UFOs—UnForgiveness Objections

If you're unwilling to forgive somebody, watch out! You think your offender has problems? That person's problems are nothing compared to the hot water you could find yourself in. For one thing, you will end up unforgiven—guaranteed! The Bible says that if we refuse to forgive others, the Lord will refuse to forgive us.

Almost as bad, you'll find yourself locked up in a kind of prison that you've created. When you refuse to forgive someone, the bitterness in your heart places you in bondage to the offender. You end up thinking about the other person so much that you're as good as chained to the individual. You obsess, you burn; it's not pretty. The moment you truly forgive, however, you set yourself free from your self-imposed prison and open up your own life to the forgiveness God has for you.

A forgiving heart is the key that opens up the cell you've locked yourself in.

Be ever careful in your choice
of friends, and let your special
love be given to those whose
strength of character may prove
the whip that drives you
ever to fair Wisdom's goal.

*Don't make friends with people
who have hot, violent tempers.
You might learn their habits
and not be able to change.*

PROVERBS 22:24-25 TEV

A Raging Relationship

More than likely you know at least a couple of kids who live in a constant state of rage. Anger taken to the extreme of rage has become frighteningly common, for a host of reasons. But knowing the reason a person is filled with rage is of little help when you're on the receiving end of the outburst. What you need is help, and you need it *now*.

At the first sign of rage in a friend, back off. You need to seriously reconsider the future of your relationship. Even if you feel you still have an open ear with the person, proceed with the greatest caution. You really need to keep your distance, although never abandoning your concern and compassion. The danger is not only physical but also spiritual; anger is highly infectious. Drop the friendship, but continually bring your friend before God in prayer.

Anger is only an invitation to trouble.

Dost thou love life?
Then do not squander
time, for that is the
stuff life is made of.

*A lazy person is as bad as
someone who is destructive.*

PROVERBS 18:9 TEV

Help Wanted

It's hard not to be a clock-watcher sometimes—especially when it's the last class of the day or it's the last hour of your shift at work. All you want to do is to get out as soon as possible; so you stare at the clock, trying to will it to move a little faster.

The only cure for a seemingly interminable wait is to keep yourself occupied. When your mind is completely focused on a task or project, your sense of time seems to be distorted; the minutes and hours appear to practically fly by. That may be a difficult challenge in a boring class, depending upon your teacher; but there's little excuse for not rising to the challenge at work. Without a doubt, your boss would welcome your offer to go above and beyond your job description in order to make the time pass more quickly.

Find creative ways to keep your mind and hands occupied.

Every oak tree started out
as a couple of nuts who
stood their ground.

Fools say to themselves,
"There is no God!"

PSALM 14:1 TEV

Uh, Uh, Uh!

How do you respond to an atheist? Do you quote Scripture and get into an argument–or do you shrink back, wishing you could send in the professional Bible scholars, so you could go hide? Well, neither approach is going to make a favorable impression on your atheist friend. When you do get into a discussion, remember that your purpose is not to win an argument but to win a soul to a life of faith. That person's spiritual need comes before everything else. Being loving comes before being right.

Before you came to faith in God, you probably had some serious doubts–and if you were allowed to express those doubts openly, you know what a priceless gift that was. Give that same gift to your atheist or agnostic friends. And don't feel as if you have to have all the answers; your testimony is your strongest ally.

Admitting you don't have all the answers underscores your honesty.

The only way to have
a friend is to be one.

Love one another with brotherly
affection—as members of one
family—giving precedence and
showing honor to one another.

ROMANS 12:10 AMP

"There You Are," Not "Here I Am."

It's hard under any circumstances to make new friends, and it can seem impossible for kids who are forced to move to a new town or state. Enroll in a new school in the middle of the year, and you'd might as well wear a neon sign identifying yourself as a loser.

One of the biggest mistakes kids make in situations like this is to exaggerate about their lives. They try to draw attention to themselves by making up a more exotic past than they actually lived. "My brother is part of *NSYNC." But those kinds of lies always backfire; even if the dishonesty isn't discovered, they annoy the other kids. A far better tactic is to take a genuine interest in others—if you ask questions and seek information from them, you show yourself to be exactly the opposite of the know-it-all that nobody can stand.

Making another person feel important is a great way to make a friend.

The greatest mistake you can make in life is to be continually fearing you will make one.

Be strong and courageous. Do not be afraid or terrified because of them, for the L<small>ORD</small> your God goes with you; he will never leave you nor forsake you.

Life on the Edge

Have you ever looked at certain people and wondered how they could stand to live such a boring existence? You probably even think that about your own parents, aunts, and uncles. And you decide that there's no way you'll ever end up like that. You might be surprised, though, at the number of people who faced their future with the same resolve you have—yet find themselves just going through the motions of life now.

What makes the difference? Courage. Simple, fearless living. Daring to risk making a mistake instead of daring nothing and getting nothing. Asking God what to do and then doing it—no questions asked. You want life on the edge? If your exposure to a life of faith is anything less than that, then maybe you haven't seen the genuine article—because living for God is the ultimate in extreme living.

Don't just go through the motions—
go through the fire with God.

Vision is the art of seeing things invisible.

By faith, [Abraham] left Egypt, not fearing the king's anger; he persevered because he saw him who is invisible.

HEBREWS 11:27

Lose Your Mind

Has anyone ever accused you of seeing things? In some circles, that's one way of asking if you've lost your mind. Well . . . have you? If you've been consciously transforming your mind with God's Word, then in a sense you *are* losing your mind—the mind that formerly viewed everything without an understanding of God's purpose for man. Your renewed mind sees things differently, and it sees things that many other people cannot see.

When a sudden tragedy strikes, you see a hopeful future despite your tears. When a friend is weighed down by sin, you see an open door leading to repentance and salvation. When violence hits your neighborhood, you see the prospect of turning the focus of the people toward spiritual things. That's seeing things with a renewed mind. We can see the activity of God in the lives of those around us.

It takes eyes of faith to see the invisible.

Defer not till tomorrow to be wise; tomorrow's sun to thee may never rise.

Make level paths for your feet and take only ways that are firm. Do not swerve to the right or the left; keep your foot from evil.

PROVERBS 4:26-27

The Race Is On

Think of your life as a cross-country trip; your long-range goal is your destination at the other end, but there are a million side trips you could make along the way. It takes wisdom to interpret the signposts. To truly enjoy the journey, you don't want to barrel straight through—but which stops will refresh and energize you? Which will lure and entrap you?

Along with the wisdom God has given you, your greatest companion on the journey of life is your conscience—that little voice inside your head and heart that says no: don't do this, don't go there, don't take this pathway, don't trust that person. As long as you keep your focus on God, you can trust your conscience—one of the means He uses to speak to you—to "keep your foot from evil."

Side trips can provide needed relaxation—just make sure they lead back to the main road.

Study without reflection is a waste of time; reflection without study is dangerous.

Do not let this Book of the Law depart from your mouth; meditate on it day and night, so that you may be careful to do everything written in it. Then you will be prosperous and successful.

JOSHUA 1:8

Study Hall

Study! You're already overloaded with stuff to study, and now people expect you to add the Bible on top of all that! Look at it this way: few other subjects that you are required to study today are guaranteed to be of use every day of your life, for as long as you live. The Bible can make that guarantee.

Knowing how to study the Bible is critical to its usefulness. Studying it without ever allowing its truth to seep into your heart through meditation and reflection is pointless. As you read the Bible, keep your mind and your heart open to the riches it contains. Concentrate on what you're reading to determine how to apply the words on the page to the life that you live. Be careful to follow through and do what it says.

Meditating on Scripture is simply thinking deeply about what is contained in the Word of God.

Wise men are not always silent, but they know when to be.

Your speech should always be pleasant.

Colossians 4:6 TEV

Will Work for a Pizza and a Smile

It seems that most kids today have an after-school or weekend job. No doubt, it's a bottom-rung job, one that involves a fair degree of dirty work and drudgery. Plenty of kids recognize this as a fact of life and are grateful for their paychecks, even if they're not too crazy about what they had to do to earn them.

One of the most irritating aspects of an entry-level job is the inevitable coworker who complains about everything under the sun—sometimes, they've got it better than you do! They spend so much time complaining about the conditions and arguing about who's responsible for what, that they seem to manage to get through an entire shift without doing any real work. Be his counterpart—the one whose uncomplaining, good-natured attitude makes your workplace a pleasant place to be.

The less you complain, the more you'll be able to enjoy your job.

True friends stab
you in the front.

*If one falls down, his friend
can help him up. But pity
the man who falls and has
no one to help him up!*

ECCLESIASTES 4:10

A Friend in Your Face

It's almost strange the way we make friends. Why do we click with some kids and not with others—others who are just as friendly, share the same interests, and seem to like us? It's as if there's an unseen quality some kids have that creates a special bond with us. A friend like that is one we can count on to cheer us up when we're depressed, defend us when we're attacked, and comfort us when we're hurting.

A friend like that also has the guts to confront us when we're not living the right way. Even while giving us a major talking-to, we know this person is doing it out of love and concern. And even if we ignore their advice, they'll be there to help us pick up the pieces if we end up broken and shattered.

A true friend cares enough to confront us when we're wrong.

One must have a good memory to be able to keep the promises one makes.

Whatever your lips utter you must be sure to do, because you made your vow freely to the LORD your God with your own mouth.

DEUTERONOMY 23:23

A Promise Is a Promise Is a Promise

Making a vow to God is a serious matter. He's merciful and quick to forgive, but we should never take lightly the promises we make to Him. He has this habit of taking us at our word and reminding us about it. Have you ever been in a bind and promised God that if He'd only get you out of the mess, you'd serve Him forever? Well, He has a long memory!

In a more serious vein, it grieves the heart of God when we break vows. Many loving couples who have made vows to stand by each other through sickness and poverty have broken those vows over far less cause. Sometimes parents break vows to bring up their children according to biblical principles. Although God forgives those who confess their failings, broken vows dishonor Him, the One who never breaks His promises.

Start now. Commit yourself to integrity. Keep your promises to God and to your friends.

Don't make promises you can't keep— to God or anyone else.

Money is like promises—
easier made than kept.

*Whoever trusts in his riches
will fall, but the righteous will
thrive like a green leaf.*

PROVERBS 11:28

Money Doesn't Grow on Trees

Do you almost wish you could be a little kid again, thinking that a dollar is a really big deal? Maybe, but the sooner you get a handle on the wise use of money, the better off you'll be.

Money is a necessity, and one that can do a tremendous amount of good. In itself, money is not evil; it's the *love* of money that the Bible calls the root of all evil. That's one reason why reporters are trained to follow the money: In any crime or political scandal, it's often the love of money and the power it represents that cause people to go wrong.

For most of us, the problem is simply managing the money we have—or don't have. Start now, before you have any more responsibilities, to follow this proven formula: give at least ten percent, save ten percent, invest ten percent, and live off the rest.

Use money—don't place your trust in it.

O wisdom of the world!
O strength of the world!
The humblest feeblest
Christian has that which
is impossible to you!

*Nothing is impossible
with God.*

LUKE 1:37

Frog Me, Baby

History is filled with stories of people who did the seemingly impossible, even as others were telling them they couldn't. The wisest people quietly went on with their work, ignoring the critics and mockers, and succeeded in accomplishing what others could not conceive.

We see the same things happening today, only in a fraction of the time. Now, new technology makes creating the uncreatable possible in a matter of months. It takes single-minded people, who are willing to put on the blinders and concentrate their time and energy on the task at hand despite the mocking or discouraging words.

The Bible warns about the danger of being double-minded when God asks for the impossible. We *can* accomplish the impossible—when God is in it, through it, and all around it. Nothing less than "FROG"—Fully Relying On God—will do. That's faith.

*Got detractors? Quietly keep going
and trusting until you succeed.*

If we could read the secret history of our enemies, we should find in each man's life sorrow and suffering enough to disarm all hostility.

How much better to get wisdom than gold! And to get understanding is to be chosen rather than silver.

PROVERBS 16:16 NKJV

But Whyyyy?

You probably started asking *why* as a toddler and haven't stopped. The *why* of things intrigues us, particularly when we can't see any logical reason for what we've just been asked—or told—to do. While it may not be the smartest question, it doesn't hurt to keep asking.

Knowing *why* helps you understand human nature. If a friend suddenly withdraws, you may feel abandoned, until you discover that his family is falling apart and he can't handle being around normal kids. Knowing *why* churches follow certain rituals helps you understand the rich meaning behind traditions that made no sense to you before.

Before you rush to judge your teacher, employer, family, and friends, stop and ask why they may have certain expectations of you. You may disagree with their thinking, but you'll acquire a habit that will help you all through your life.

A why that sounds like a whine
quickly loses its value.

Never allow your sense of
self to become associated
with your sense of job.
If your job vanishes,
your self doesn't.

*What advantage does man have
in all his work Which he does
under the sun? A generation
goes and a generation comes,
But the earth remains forever.*

ECCLESIASTES 1:3-4 NASB

Me, Myself, and I

There you are at the beach, soaking up the rays and attracting the hottest dates around. Life is good, really good. From your oceanside lifeguard perch, you look out over your sunny domain and know that you *rule*.

Then you lose your job. No more sun, surf, or fawning admirers. You need money, but the best you can find is a job stocking grocery shelves. Life looks bad, really bad.

Unless you're careful, you may find yourself sinking into depression. But your problem isn't your new job; it's the identity you lost with your old job. You are not your job or the activities you do. Those things will change, but you will be living with yourself a long time. Make sure you're the kind of person you'd want to live with—no matter what you are doing.

Remember—regardless of where you go in life, you'll have to take yourself along.

Smart is believing
half of what you hear;
brilliant is knowing
which half to believe.

Wisdom and truth will enter
the very center of your being,
filling your life with joy.

PROVERBS 2:10 TLB

Wisdom Rocks

If wisdom and truth fill you with joy, then foolishness and deceit will fill you with misery. When wisdom and truth get mixed in with foolishness and deceit, it takes a brilliant mind to sort it all out.

The daily newspaper is covered with that kind of jumbled thinking. Many politicians, business leaders, and others have become experts at making deception sound like truth and foolishness sound like wisdom. You can train yourself to see through the smokescreens, though. One way is by questioning everything you hear and read. If you keep an open mind, that's not cynicism—it's a smart way of living.

A second way is by judging everything against the backdrop of the truth that is revealed in Scripture. That truth is unchanging, and it will always steer you in the right direction—one that will fill your life with joy.

*K*eep the "center of your being" free
from foolishness and deceit.

Be thou as chaste as ice,
as pure as snow.

*Marriage should be
honored by all, and the
marriage bed kept pure.*

HEBREWS 13:4

The Right Place for Sex

Sex outside of marriage has become a life-or-death issue, though your friends may try to convince you that only adults are uptight about sex. That argument just doesn't wash anymore. Many of today's adults are the ones who ushered in the whole sexual revolution, and many have lived to regret it.

Having sex too soon and with too many partners has ruined the lives of many people. Not just your peers—like the ones who need to find babysitters during the school day—and those with life-threatening, sexually transmitted diseases, but also adults whose sexual past has affected their current relationship with their spouse. They've learned some irreversible lessons the hard way, and they're trying to spare you a lifetime of pain. That has nothing to do with being uptight and every-thing to do with loving you and caring about you.

Sacrificing pleasure today may save your marriage in the future.

Folks who never do any
more than they get paid
for, never get paid for
any more than they do.

"Many . . . have done well,
But you exceed them all."

PROVERBS 31:29 NKJV

You—Need to Stand Out

You may need to look at your job in a whole new way, even if it's the most menial job in a place of business that's full of menial jobs. Everyone seems to make fun of the burger-flipper, but if that's you, it doesn't feel much like a joke, does it?

Nevertheless, place your mark of excellence on everything you do. If your only job is as a student, then that's where you need to excel. Even if you're not academically oriented, you can be an exemplary student. Maybe you baby-sit some neighborhood kids after school or you're a cashier at Wal-Mart; there's no reason why you can't put your signature on those jobs as well. You can be a standout—but not if you look down on your job. Look up and find a way to make a lasting, positive impression where you work.

Make sure your self-portrait at work shows your best side.

The man who is born with a talent which he is meant to use finds his greatest happiness in using it.

Life is worth nothing unless I use it for doing the work assigned me by the Lord Jesus.

ACTS 20:24 TLB

Fulfill Your Destiny

So just what is the work assigned to you? You may not know what it is now, but you probably have a pretty good idea what your strengths and talents are. Well-meaning friends and family may try to influence your career choice, but you are the one who will have to live with it for a long time. A more lucrative career may in fact be an inferior route for you; an enviable paycheck is no match for the satisfaction of knowing that you're doing exactly what you were put on Earth to do.

Deep down inside, we all want to believe that our lives count for something. The best way to insure that is to spend time looking at all those things you're good at and are passionate about and then laying it all out before God. He'll help you pick out those interests that will endure.

Building your career on your strengths will take you through the long haul.

It's one of the hardest things
in the world to accept
criticism . . . and turn
it to your advantage.

*No chastening seems to be
joyful for the present, but
grievous; nevertheless, afterward
it yields the peaceable fruit
of righteousness to those who
have been trained by it.*

HEBREWS 12:11 NKJV

Invite Criticism

Some days it seems as if you can't do anything right, at least where some people are concerned. They'll criticize you for the way you look, how loud your music is, what you had for lunch, and where you were last night. Look at it this way—they must think you're one fascinating human being to spend so much time noticing every little thing about you.

Other people offer genuinely constructive criticism in an effort to help you find your way in this world. They see your potential, and they know you can go further in life.

Examine the motives of your critics: are they to cut you down or to build you up? Ignore the former, but pay close attention to the latter. Even if you disagree with their criticism, pretend—for just a moment—that they're right and decide whether their suggestions could improve your life. You may thank them in the long run.

Agreeing with a well-intentioned critic doesn't always have to hurt.

You must have long-range
goals to keep you from
being frustrated by
short-range failures.

*The vision is yet for
an appointed time . . .
Though it tarries, wait for it;
Because it will surely come.*

HABAKKUK 2:3 NKJV

He Shoots, He Scores!

Right now your focus is probably set squarely on those things that lie right in front of you: getting good grades, doing well in sports, or getting the right date for the prom. Maybe you have a few long-range goals, but if you're like most kids, those goals are kind of fuzzy. Perhaps you want to be a software designer, a professional athlete, or a well-known actor. In order for your immediate goals to make more sense, it helps to narrow down the focus of your long-range goals.

Ask yourself questions: Whose work do you admire in the field in which you want to work? Which companies or teams or restaurants look most like the one with whom you'd like to be involved? If you can answer that, it will help you know what you're actually working toward and where you should concentrate your energy right now.

What you do today is like a deposit in a savings account for your future goals.

Genius, in truth, means
little more than the
faculty of perceiving
in an unhabitual way.

*Look with your eyes and hear
with your ears and pay
attention to everything
I am going to show you.*

EZEKIEL 40:4

Intense Power

Did you know that you can increase your powers of observation? Law enforcement, military, and security personnel know that intense observation is a critical skill that can be learned and refined over a lifetime. Even if you're not training to work in a dangerous environment, you can improve your ability to observe the details around you that others might easily miss. What's the point, though? For Diane Sawyer, the answer is obvious: it made her a better reporter. But what about the rest of us?

Paying close attention to detail makes us better students and better employees—and possibly in the future, better employers. It will make us better parents and spouses someday. And most important, it makes us better *people* today, the kind who notice and comment on the little things in others that make them feel set apart and special.

Train yourself in the habit of paying attention.
You'll learn a great deal.

The lightning spark of Thought generated . . . in the solitary mind, awakens its express likeness in another mind, in a thousand other minds, and all blaze up together in combined fire.

Watch over your heart with all diligence, For from it flow the springs of life.

PROVERBS 4:23 NASB

Take Us to Your Leader

Mind control. Sounds like something out of a science fiction novel. It happens every day, just not in the futuristic, sinister way we have been conditioned to look for. People can be persuaded, pressured, manipulated, desensitized, and, yes, conditioned to think a certain way. Subtle efforts to control our minds come at us from all directions.

Protect your mind from the control of others, not by closing it but by opening it. As long as you have surrendered your mind—and all that you are—to God, then you can confidently examine and weigh all that you're exposed to against the truth. Closing your mind only makes you incapable of passing that truth along to people who would consider you to be clueless. Opening it makes you more discerning and skilled at unmasking those who would attempt to coerce you into thinking their way.

Guard your mind as carefully as you guard your heart.

People may doubt
what you say, but they
will always believe
what you do.

*The tree is known and
recognized and judged
by its fruit.*

Matthew 12:33 amp

Walkie-Talkie

It's called "walking the talk"—practicing what you preach. You can talk until you're blue in the face, but if your actions contradict what you say, you've wasted your breath.

If you tell others they should give their time and money to a cause, you'd better be prepared to do it too. If you speak with great sorrow and passion about the plight of the poor and homeless, you need to make sure you're the one ladling out the soup at the local mission. And if you're going to preach the Good News, you certainly better be living it out, for all to see.

Words are never scarce. Unfortunately, actions to back up those words are. If all those who moralize would live according to the high moral standards they espouse, we'd have a different and better world. Be one of the comparatively few whose words and actions are one and the same—and thus make your words more believable.

Maintain your credibility by putting your words into action.

If you don't think
about the future, you
cannot have one.

Aim for perfection.

2 Corinthians 13:11

Target Practice

Do you have high aspirations, a desire for something so out there that even you know it would take nothing short of a miracle to accomplish it? Congratulations! You've given yourself something so lofty to shoot for that you can't possibly do it by yourself—and that's good news. Astronauts never would have set foot on the moon if it hadn't been for the thousands of people who helped them get there.

So what are you aiming for? Set your sights high, and keep your faith well maintained with plenty of prayer. Surround yourself with people who can help you hit your target, just as you help them achieve their objectives. When your spirits start to sag—and they will—ask yourself that well-known question: what's the worst that could happen? So you miss your goal . . . but you could hit something so close to it that you're thrilled beyond measure.

The future is as bright as the promises of God.

Go west, young man.

"Ask, and you will receive;
seek, and you will find;
knock, and the door
will be opened to you."

MATTHEW 7:7 TEV

The Opportunity of a Lifetime

It's sad to hear an older person lament their past: "I would have gone to college, if I'd only had the opportunity." In some cases they simply let opportunities slip by. And, as lots of people will attest to, sometimes you just have to go out and find opportunity for yourself.

How do you do that? By being alert, with all your senses tuned to what's going on around you. The simplest comment made in passing could provide the opportunity of a lifetime. Now that nearly every person in America has at least the possibility of logging on to the Internet, there's really no excuse to claim ignorance. Every major school, organization, and business has a Web site with a vast amount of information on scholarships, internships, overseas studies, and employment. Take advantage of this incredible resource—that's the twenty-first century way of making your own opportunity.

Become a relentless sleuth in search of the limitless possibilities for your life.

Being at peace with
yourself is a direct result of
finding peace with God.

*Through Christ, God made
peace between us and himself,
and God gave us the work
of telling everyone about the
peace we can have with him.*

2 CORINTHIANS 5:18 NCV

Give Me a Peace

You've probably heard the question asked in cinematic deathbed scenes or even in real life: "Has he made his peace with God?" Have you ever wondered what that really means? You may not realize it, but if you're not at peace with God, you are in a struggle against Him. Finding peace with Him is simply becoming reconciled to God through a conscious, personal relationship with His Son.

Once we've established that peace with God, we can finally make peace with ourselves. You didn't know you were struggling with yourself? Anytime you have felt a restless unhappiness with your life, you have been fighting against the person you are under the veneer you present to others. When we come to terms with God, He reveals our true nature and equips us to make those changes we've known we should make all along.

Become reconciled not only to God but also to yourself.

Quiet minds cannot be
perplexed or frightened, but
go on in fortune or misfortune
at their own private pace, like
a clock in a thunderstorm.

By the grace of God I am what I
am, and his grace to me was not
without effect. No, I worked harder
than all of them—yet not I, but
the grace of God that was with me.

1 CORINTHIANS 15:10

Duck Lessons

If you've ever seen ducks swimming, you know the picture of serenity they present. They glide through the water so effortlessly that it looks as if the current is carrying them along. Then you realize there's no current. The work of propelling them through the pond is all taking place beneath the surface.

Remember those ducks the next time you start to get rattled at work, in class, or on the basketball court. Maintaining a calm demeanor will help you think more clearly and push through the situation that's got you so ruffled.

Especially in a sports competition, you don't want your opponent to know that he's gotten to you! The most highly respected athletes and coaches are those who seldom show any negative emotion during a game.

Keep cool on the outside, but paddle furiously on the inside as you work through your strategy.

Let the world see you gliding effortlessly through the pressures of life.

We are made strong by
the difficulties we face,
not by those we evade.

*In all these things we are
more than conquerors
through him who loved us.*

ROMANS 8:37

The Courage Connection

Two soldiers hit the battlefield scared to death of what their opponents had in store for them. One faces the enemy head on, the second shrinks back. Both survive—but only one emerges with genuine strength of character. The difference is the courage the first soldier discovered only after he confronted his adversary.

It's normal to want to get out of a difficult situation. Some of the circumstances in which we find ourselves make us want to run and hide in hopes that our troubles will go away. Our weakness in the face of our problems, however, will continue to dog us.

Many people will never know how tough they are, simply because they keep avoiding hard situations. Don't you want to find out what you're made of? Toughen yourself up by facing your problems head on.

Hard times come to everyone, but not everyone conquers them.

Be wisely worldly,
be not worldly wise.

*He who trusts in himself
is a fool, but he who walks
in wisdom is kept safe.*

PROVERBS 28:26

The Mother Lode

Schooling offers a great many promised results, but wisdom is not among them. If it's acquired at all through education, wisdom is an accidental by-product obtained more by the innate, perceptive nature of the student than from any course of instruction.

No course can teach you the essence of wisdom, which is the ability to exercise unusual discernment in decision-making and in dealing with other people. You acquire it by reading and meditating on the one living book, the Bible. This doesn't mean a superficial reading, by any means, but a deep, thoughtful reading, with your mind fully engaged and your spirit fully open to the things of God. Add a willingness to be transformed and to act on what you've learned, and you've got a winning formula for obtaining wisdom and understanding. Like a miner who's just discovered the mother lode, you'll never regret the effort.

Seek out wisdom as if you're searching for a perfect diamond.

Our shadow selves, our influence, may fall where we ourselves can never be.

The only letter I need is you yourselves! . . . They can see that you are a letter from Christ, written by us . . . not one carved on stone, but in human hearts.

2 CORINTHIANS 3:2-3 TLB

Who Are You?

Some people live their lives as if they're building a monument to themselves, like the rock 'n' roll legend who tried to insist that a life-size bronze statue of himself be placed in front of the Rock and Roll Hall of Fame. Being inducted was not enough; he felt he deserved prominent exposure.

You have a greater monument to build—a lasting, positive influence on the lives of others. Unlike a bronze statue, that kind of monument can be passed around to affect the lives of countless other people as well as passed down to innumerable generations to come. Your name may not live on in concrete, marble, or bronze, but it will live on in the hearts of those you have loved and helped lead to a life with God—and it will live on in the eternal hall of fame.

Your life is a letter of faith to the waiting world around you.

When you have
accomplished your daily
task, go to sleep in peace;
God is awake.

*I will turn the darkness into
light before them and make
the rough places smooth.*

ISAIAH 42:16

Shudder and Shake

If you've just graduated or are about to, you may be experiencing a shudder of fear, now that you're faced with the reality that practically everything familiar to you is about to change. For thirteen years, you've followed a certain routine, one generally set to the rhythms of the school year and the school day. Even if you're going on to college, the school year will be about the only familiar facet of your life.

Though your future is indeed unknown to you, knowing, trusting, and understanding the nature of God gives you an edge over other kids. Not only can you move forward with complete confidence, but you also can bring others alongside you and help steer them in the one direction that's sure and dependable. You, and they, will find that no one need fear when they've placed their future in God's trustworthy hands.

You can't understand everything, but you can trust the One who does.

Do not follow where
the path may lead. Go
instead where there is no
path and leave a trail.

*Your ears shall hear a
word behind you, saying,
"This is the way, walk in it."*

ISAIAH 30:21 NKJV

Trailblazers Urgently Needed

A trailblazer is a person who creates a path through the wilderness and leaves blazes, or markers, to show those who follow which way to go. Without skilled trailblazers, it would have taken much longer to settle our country, and many a weekend hiker today would end up traveling in frustrating circles. In more serious situations, a person could be lost for so long that once they're found, it's too late.

Don't make life a frustrating, never-ending series of circles that seem to lead nowhere for others. Blaze your own trail—but leave markers behind for others to follow. Whether you prove to be a scientific wizard who creates life-changing technology, a medical researcher who discovers a life-saving breakthrough, or a parent who stumbles onto a life-altering method of controlling a two-year-old's tantrums, make sure you leave a clear pattern of discovery.

Walk through life with such authority that your trail will not fade into obscurity.

When men are rightly
occupied, their amusement
grows out of their work,
as the color-petals out
of a fruitful flower.

*This is what I have seen to be good:
it is fitting to eat and drink
and find enjoyment in all the
toil with which one toils under
the sun the few days of the life
God gives us; for this is our lot.*

ECCLESIASTES 5:18 NRSV

Taking Care of Business

Think about never having to work another day for the rest of your life! Most millionaires don't even have that kind of luxury, since it takes work to manage that amount of money or to keep on top of the people you've hired to manage it for you. The key here is finding out what you love to do and building your career around that.

If you're having trouble visualizing work as fun, start paying attention to people who seem to have a blast at work, who have as much energy at the end of the day as they did at the beginning and could keep going for the sheer enjoyment of it. That's very different from a workaholic, whose compulsion to work is unhealthy. People who love their work are those who have found the niche that was carved out especially for them.

When you find pleasure in your work, your life radiates joy.

He has achieved success
who has lived well,
laughed often,
and loved much.

*Being cheerful keeps you
healthy. It is slow death
to be gloomy all the time.*

PROVERBS 17:22 TEV

Live, Love, Laugh

Did you know there's a direct connection between your health and your frame of mind? Cheerful people are generally healthier and recover more quickly when they do suffer illness or injury. Not only that, they live longer, act and look younger. Not convinced? Think of the cheerful adults you know; their spirits are light, and they seem infused with energy and enthusiasm.

God himself is cheerful, and why His people aren't more like Him in that respect is a mystery. Who on Earth would want to be like some of His professed servants, those who walk around with long faces and point the finger of judgment at others? You can be instrumental in changing the way people view God by showing the side of Him we know to be true—the joyful aspect that drew us to Him. Let your cheerfulness serve as a magnet for others as well.

Live, love, laugh, and be happy.

Success seems to be largely
a matter of hanging on
after others have let go.

*Let us hold fast the
confession of our hope
without wavering, for He
who promised is faithful.*

HEBREWS 10:23 NKJV

And I Mean No Wavering

When clergyman Jan Hus was told he would be burned at the stake for sharing his faith, he went right on telling others the Good News. Then he started holding his hand over a candle so that he would become accustomed to the pain before the sentence was carried out. Now *that's* "holding fast . . . without wavering." To him, success meant ending his life still strong in his faith.

That kind of tenacity is called staying power—the ability, courage, and willingness to hang on to what you know is right. It takes guts to have staying power when you're by yourself, taking the heat and the consequences all alone. You won't know if you have that kind of tenacity until the time arrives; but in the meantime you need to come to an unwavering conclusion, that even if no one joins you, you will hang on.

A firm decision to persevere can compensate for a host of disadvantages.

A great deal of good can
be done in the world if
one is not too careful
who gets the credit.

Whether you eat or drink, or
whatever you may do, do all for
the honor and glory of God.

1 CORINTHIANS 10:31 AMP

No Guts No Glory

We'd probably all be surprised if we knew the number of times inventions and technological advances were slowed or sabotaged by envy. Two researchers working on similar projects are often more likely to undermine each other's work than share information. The reasons are obvious: money and ego. The one who is credited with the breakthrough gets the money and the accolades.

In your own world, you'd probably be amazed at how much could be accomplished if no one was out for individual glory. Maybe you've seen it in sports competitions or school plays; one student out for personal gain ruins the team's chances for victory or the cast's hopes for a top-notch production. Without those show-offs looking to get the credit, the team or cast would stand a better chance for success. There's nothing wrong with getting the credit you've earned—just don't seek it.

*Save the glory for the only
One who deserves it.*

All work, even
cotton-spinning is noble.

You have been faithful and
trustworthy over a little; I will
put you in charge of much.

MATTHEW 25:21 AMP

Invest in Your Future Today

Do you have delusions—visions of grandeur? You know, a picture of your future that includes an annual income of millions of dollars or more, most of which would be used to promote world peace and eliminate world hunger, of course. Maybe you'd establish a world-wide missions organization that would send out thousands of missionaries to minister to the lost and needy in faraway countries. Sounds great, doesn't it?

Well . . . what are you doing *today* to support missions, feed the hungry, and foster world peace? Do you offer money to an outreach or canned goods to the poor or compromise in a family conflict? These are ways of being faithful and trustworthy over a little.

Remember, too, that God loves to use little things to accomplish big things. Give Him the little that you have control over, and He'll use it for His glory.

David proved his military competence by using five smooth stones—very effectively.

Every Christian needs half an hour of prayer each day, except when he is busy. Then he needs an hour.

Evening and morning
and at noon I will pray,
and cry aloud, And
He shall hear my voice.

PSALM 55:17 NKJV

Prayer Can Make or Break Your Day

Church reformer Martin Luther is said to have spent hours in prayer every morning. That alone is pretty impressive, but here's the kicker: when he was facing an unusually busy day, Luther would spend *twice* as much time in prayer. Wouldn't it make more sense to get on with his day? Your answer to that question could reveal a lot about how you see prayer.

Luther knew that the more responsibilities he took on, the more he needed to rely on God. But he never for a minute believed his many hours and his many words in prayer would impress God. No, prayer was meant to change *him,* not impress God or change His mind. And by laying out his daily schedule before God, he showed his willingness to have those plans changed.

Our plans will be effective only to the extent that we rely on God as we make them.

Expect great things *from* God. Attempt great things *for* God.

"Truly, truly, I say to you, he who believes in Me, the works that I do, he will do also; and greater works than these he will do; because I go to the Father."

JOHN 14:12 NASB

Imagine the Unimaginable

What do you expect from God? Health, wealth, a happy and safe life? The love of a beautiful girl or handsome guy? Try for something even bigger and better than all that: expect Him to use you in such a powerful way that you can't even envision it right now. That's a pretty significant thing to trust Him for—the unimaginable.

Now, what great things do you plan to attempt for God? That might be easier. Maybe you plan to share the Gospel with your friends or go on a short-term missions trip. You may even feel called to full-time missions work, the pastoral ministry, or worship team ministry. Whatever it is you're planning, merge your goals with those great expectations you have of God. Remember—He's already promised that you can do greater works than Jesus did when He was on Earth.

Let God bring the unimaginable to pass in your life.

Anybody can do their best.
God helps us to do
better than our best.

*Glory be to God who by his
mighty power at work within
us is able to do far more
than we would ever dare
to ask or even dream of.*

EPHESIANS 3:20 TLB

When Your Best Isn't Good Enough

What do we often hear people say when they've accomplished something with mediocre results? "Well, I did my best." They shrug their shoulders and walk away. Maybe you've also heard the likely retort, "Your best just isn't good enough."

It's possible that a teacher or a parent has leveled those words at you. And maybe your best *wasn't* good enough, at least not according to others. What can you do about that in the future? Give God your best and see what He'll do with it. He'll do far more than you would even *dare* to ask! That's a pretty tall order, especially if you're already comfortable with asking big things of God. Yes, you should continue to strive for excellence, but keep in mind the extra measure of miracle-working power God can add to it.

Go beyond doing things halfway. Let God amaze you with what He does with your best.

It is better to wear
out than to rust out.

*Whatever your hand
finds to do, do it
with all your might.*

ECCLESIASTES 9:10

Yaaawn

Laziness has no place in a life of faith. The Bible compares a lazy person to one who destroys—if you're not working due to laziness, you're tearing down.

Any believer who "rusts out" before he "wears out" is one who has not discovered the secret to living the abundant life: living out your faith with all your might! And you can forget about retirement—that word just isn't in the vocabulary of a true servant of God. No, a true servant would rather breathe his last as he's sharing the Gospel than be caught in a semiconscious spiritual nap.

Does that mean you'll never experience rest and relaxation? No. It means you'll never want to take a vacation from God or rest on your laurels, settling for a passive life in front of the tube. True servants are active in their faith right to the end of their lives.

The abundant life is a productive life.

Blessed is the man who,
having nothing to say,
abstains from giving in
words evidence of the fact.

There is a time for everything,
and a season for every activity
under heaven . . . a time to
be silent and a time to speak.

ECCLESIASTES 3:1-7

The Awesome Power of Silence

They say silence is golden, but if they're right, we're definitely suffering from a major gold shortage. Everybody seems to be talking. Places where people used to show respect through silence—in church or in a movie theater—are now fair game for the disrupting influence of ongoing conversations.

There's power in remaining silent—power that few people realize because they're so busy talking! All you have to do is remain silent during an animated conversation among your friends, and soon they'll all be turning to you for your opinion. After all, anyone who hasn't said anything yet must have really valuable thoughts after thinking so hard, right?

With wisdom and maturity come the ability to know when to remain silent. Silence often carries with it an authority that's far weightier than the words you *could* speak.

There are times when your silence will speak louder than your words.

Great men are they
who see that spiritual
is stronger than any
material force; that
thoughts rule the world.

*As he thinks within
himself, so he is.*

PROVERBS 23:7 NASB

Whatcha Thinkin' 'Bout?

Our thought life is powerful. Dwell on something long enough, and it's not a long walk to making it a reality in our lives. This can work for us or against us, of course. Just replace the word "something" in that sentence with a word like "pornography" to see how it works against us. That's why it's so important to be careful what we think about.

When you find yourself obsessing over things you know are wrong, or replaying an argument or negative conversation over and over again, it's time to erase the tape in your brain by recording over it. Make a conscious attempt to obsess about something right and good—seriously! It often takes significant mental effort to steer our thoughts away from those things we know we shouldn't be thinking about. But you *can* control your thoughts and the course of your life. Decide to do it today.

The shape of our thoughts determines the shape of our lives.

Conquer yourself rather
than the world.

*Encourage the young men
to be self-controlled.*

TITUS 2:6

Down, Self! Down!

Conquering our selves—the part of us that just loves to do the things contrary to what's right or good for us—is a huge step toward maturity.

Self-control begins with confession—owning up to those areas of our lives with which we continually struggle. Maybe it's food, impure thoughts, sex, substance abuse, or anger; we all know what our stumbling blocks are, but we don't always want to admit them. Well, go ahead—admit it. Then ask God to give you the strength to overcome that area of weakness.

Here's where the real test comes. It's up to you to diligently avoid situations where you know you'll meet up with your stumbling block. That may mean giving up certain routines or even friendships, but until you master your self through the power of God, your self will master you.

Your character is formed in large part by your success in mastering self-control.

Joy to forgive and
joy to be forgiven.

*Oh, what joy for those whose
rebellion is forgiven, whose
sin is put out of sight!*

PSALM 32:1 NLT

Presto! You're Clean

Maybe you're one of those kids who has already blown it—big time. If you haven't asked for God's forgiveness, stop reading this and start praying right now! He will forgive you; all you need to do is ask and then decide not to go back to that way of life. But maybe you've already experienced that forgiveness, and you're still living with regret.

Is there something you need to do to repair the damage your sin caused? Then do it—and move on. The Bible tells us that once our sin is forgiven, God forgets all about it. It would be great if we could do the same, but it seems easier to forget today's homework assignment than a past failing. Whenever that troubling memory surfaces, follow it through to its actual conclusion: the unfailing, wonderful, incredible grace of God.

At this moment, your future is absolutely spotless. Don't let your past poison your present.

All power is a trust that
we are accountable
for its exercise.

*Daniel soon showed that he could
do better work than the other
supervisors or the governors.
Because he was so outstanding,
the king considered putting him
in charge of the whole empire.*

DANIEL 6:3 TEV

In Hot Pursuit of Power

Anyone can say they're striving for excellence, but a person's motivation may not be quite so impressive. At the heart of that individual's striving is a quest for power. The desire for spiritual power—power over sin, power to pray, power to lead others to a life of faith—is one thing, but the lust for earthly power is another. That lust drives people to lie, cheat, and steal in their hot pursuit to dominate.

The quest for excellence, on the other hand, is always accompanied by integrity, because true excellence cannot exist without it. A person can be highly skilled and financially successful but a miserable failure when it comes to character. No one of inferior character can be said to have achieved excellence.

As you enter each new stage of biological maturity, make sure you carry with you the marks of emotional maturity.

If you must have power, strive for the right kind—power to do what is right.

Out of debt,
out of danger.

*Give everyone what you
owe him . . . Let no
debt remain outstanding.*

ROMANS 13:7-8

Give It to Me Now!

Have you ever heard of deferred gratification? It basically means waiting to get something you want. Its opposite—instant gratification—is one of the primary reasons people get into debt. They want something, and they want it *now*. Rather than wait until they have the money, they pull out the plastic and charge like crazy.

Maybe you don't have any plastic yet—credit cards, that is. Actually that's a good thing, because now you have the opportunity to learn how to handle money before the credit card companies start loading your mailbox with every enticing deal under the sun. They make going into debt sound so easy—which it is—and so much fun—which it isn't—once payback time comes.

Once you make the decision to avoid debt, stick to your decision—or risk experiencing misery when the bills come due.

Rather go to bed without dinner than to rise in debt.

Thru all the tumult and the strife, I hear that music ringing. It sounds and echoes in my soul; How can I keep from singing?

He put a new song in my mouth, a hymn of praise to our God.

PSALM 40:3

Let It Rip

What would you do right now if you knew you were going to suffer excruciating pain? Would you gather your friends around you and start *singing*? Probably not. Like most people, you'd probably be scared to death. Well, it doesn't have to be like that. The Bible tells us that the night before Jesus was crucified, one of the last things He did with his friends was sing to God.

Don't take life so seriously that you forget to sing through the bad times as well as the good. You can change your whole perspective on a troubling situation by listening to the song God has placed within your heart. You don't think it's there? It is—you just have to tune your spiritual ears a little better to hear. During the rough times, pull every joyful song you know out of your memory and let it rip.

Even your most out-of-tune singing
can help chase away the blues.

They're only truly great
who are truly good.

*Teach these great truths to
trustworthy men who will, in
turn, pass them on to others.*

2 TIMOTHY 2:2 TLB

Be a Darkroom— Develop Greatness in Others

There's a flip side to having a mentor, a person who's willing to teach you the ropes and guide you as you find your way in life. That flip side is *being* a mentor. Even as a teenager, you may already exhibit the characteristics of a born leader. If that's true of you, then you're in a terrific position to develop greatness in other kids.

All you need to do is share, the same thing your mother admonished you to do when you were three years old. Share your experiences, your insights, your knowledge, your resources, your contacts—whatever you've acquired that has helped you make a go of it in school, at work, or just in life. When you pass great truths along to others, you have the satisfaction of watching them move forward along their own paths to greatness.

Only a selfless person can be considered great by others.

Do all the good you can,
by all the means you can,
in all the ways you can,
in all the places you can,
at all the times you can,
to all the people you can,
as long as ever you can.

*It is more blessed to give
than to receive.*

ACTS 20:35 NASB

No Strings Attached

This is where you stop keeping score. You know—
"I did this for her, so she should do that for me." That's
giving to get, and that will never make your life an
enjoyable one. If you want to know what real peace
and contentment are, try giving just for the sake of
giving—no strings attached.

What's even better is *generous* giving just for the
sake of giving. Whether they mean to or not, some religious leaders make it sound as if the purpose of giving
is to get all kinds of blessings from God. It's true that He
loves it when His children are liberal in their giving,
and often His blessings seem to flow. What He wants,
however, is followers who give generously without a
thought about what they might get in return.

*Giving in secret is not only the noble way
to give, it's also a whole lot of fun.*

Humor is to life what
shock absorbers
are to automobiles.

*A cheerful heart has
a continual feast.*

PROVERBS 15:15 NRSV

Insert Laughter Here

Has it ever occurred to you that God has a great sense of humor? No? Well, maybe you need to meditate on a giraffe for a while—or a walrus. Or take a trip to the zoo and watch the monkeys.

What about you? Have you learned to laugh at yourself, with all your foibles, weird ways, and idiosyncrasies? If you haven't, it's high time you did, because few things will carry you through life the way the ability to laugh at yourself will. When others try to make fun of you, you'll have it all over them, because you've learned to accept yourself—warts and all.

It is important to note that genuinely funny humor is never dished out at the expense of others. Godly laughter is kind. There's enough to laugh about in life without the arrogance of ridiculing other individuals or groups.

Every bump in the road of life will hurt if you don't learn to laugh along the way.

Success is the result of
working hard, playing
hard, and keeping
your mouth shut.

*Even a fool is thought to be
wise when he is silent. It pays
him to keep his mouth shut.*

PROVERBS 17:28 TLB

Open Mouth, Insert Foot

You have to work hard to succeed. But there's one area in which you may need help—learning when not to speak. That's especially important when it comes to criticizing someone in authority over you. Undermining your boss's authority all but guarantees you a one-way pass to the company parking lot. You can disagree all you like—as long as you discuss your position with your boss privately and respectfully.

The same holds true with your pastor, a teacher, or a professor. Public criticism is never warranted and can backfire on you in a flash. If you have a grievance with someone, pray about it before you do anything, and once you get the green light in prayer, take your grievance to the proper authority. Who knows? Someday you may be the proper authority, and you'll realize how much you appreciate people like yourself.

You'll never have to take back words you've never said.

Acknowledgements

(6) Aeschylus, (8) George Herbert, (10,96,126) Thomas Carlyle, (12) Epictetus, (14) Miguel de Cervantes, (16) Robert Pollock, (18) Mary Gardiner Brainard, (20) Henry Wheeler Shaw, (22) Arthur Fredrick Sheldon, (24) Euripides, (26) Jean-Baptiste Molière, (28) Dionysius, (30) Dio Chrysostom, (32) Aubrey Thomas de Vere, (34,40,56,68, 82,88,92,98,108, 114,116,120,122,146,154) Anonymous, (36) Abbe Henri de Tourville, (38) John Boyle O'Reilly, (42) Robert J. Burdette, (44) Edgar Allan Poe, (46) Diogenes Laertius, (48) Oliver Goldsmith, (50) Pittacus, (52) Mutsuhito, (54) Benjamin Franklin, (58,138) Ralph Waldo Emerson, (60,86) Elbert G. Hubbard, (62) Jonathan Swift, (64) William Congreve, (66) Confucius, (70) Oscar Wilde, (72) Friedrich Nietzsche, (74) Henry Wheeler Shaw, (76) Cardinal John Henry Newman, (78) Henry Wadsworth Longfellow, (80,94) William James, (84) William Shakespeare, (90) Francis Bacon, (100) John Galsworthy, (101) William Carey, (102) John Soule, (104) William M. Evarts, (106) Robert Louis Stevenson, (110) Francis Quarles, (112) Anna Hamilton, (118) John Ruskin, (121) Harry Woods, (124) The Jesuits, (128) Catherine Booth, (130) William Carey, (132) Edward Young, (134) Richard Cumberland, (136) George Eliot, (140) René Descartes, (142) Richard Garnett, (144) Benjamin Disraeli, (147) Benjamin Franklin, (148) The Quakers, (150) George Chapman, (152) John Wesley, (156) G.K. Chesterton.

References

Unless otherwise indicated, all Scripture quotations are taken from the *Holy Bible, New International Version*® NIV®. Copyright © 1973, 1978, 1984 by International Bible Society. Used by permission of Zondervan Publishing House. All rights reserved.

Scripture quotations marked AMP are taken from *The Amplified Bible, New Testament.* Copyright © 1958, 1987 by The Lockman Foundation, La Habra, California. Used by permission.

Scripture quotations marked NASB are taken from the *New American Standard Bible.* Copyright © The Lockman Foundation 1960, 1962, 1963, 1968, 1971, 1972, 1973, 1975, 1977, 1995. Used by permission.

Scriptures marked NCV are quoted from *The Holy Bible, New Century Version,* copyright © 1987, 1988, 1991 by Word Publishing, Dallas, Texas 75039. Used by permission.

Scripture quotations marked NKJV are taken from *The New King James Version.* Copyright © 1979, 1980, 1982, 1994, Thomas Nelson, Inc.

Scripture quotations marked TEV are from the *Today's English Version – Second Edition* © 1992 by American Bible Society. Used by permission.

Verses marked TLB are taken from *The Living Bible* © 1971 © 1986. Used by permission of Tyndale House Publishers, Inc., Wheaton, Illinois 60189. All rights reserved.

Scripture quotation marked NLT are taken from the *Holy Bible, New Living Translation,* copyright © 1996. Used by permission of Tyndale House Publishers, Inc., Wheaton, Illinois 60189. All rights reserved.

Additional copies of this book and other
titles from Honor Books
are available from your local bookstore.

Also Available:

E-mail from God for Teens
God's Little Devotional Book for Teens
God's Little Lessons for Teens
God Speaks Stories for Teens
In the Chat Room with God
More E-mail from God for Teens
My Personal Promise Bible for Teens
Real Teens, Real Stories, Real Life

If you have enjoyed this book,
or if it has impacted your life,
we would like to hear from you.

Please contact us at:

Honor Books
Department E
P.O. Box 55388
Tulsa, Oklahoma 74155
Or by e-mail at *info@honorbooks.com*